I0813464

The Essential Kay Smith

The Essential Kay Smith

selected by Michael Oliver

The Porcupine's Quill

Library and Archives Canada Cataloguing in Publication

Title: The essential Kay Smith / selected by Michael Oliver.
Other titles: Poems. Selections
Names: Smith, Kay, 1911–2004, author. | Oliver, Michael, 1946– editor.
Series: Essential poets (Erin, Ont.) ; 20.
Description: Series statement: Essential poets series ; 20 | Poems.
Identifiers: Canadiana 20190155280 | ISBN 9780889844261 (softcover)
Classification: LCC PS8537.M62 A6 2019 | DDC C811/.54—dc23

1 2 3 • 21 20 19

Published by The Porcupine's Quill, 68 Main Street, PO Box 160,
Erin, Ontario NOB 1T0. http://porcupinesquill.ca

Copyedited by Chandra Wohleber.
Represented in Canada by Canadian Manda.
Trade orders are available from University of Toronto Press.

We acknowledge the support of the Ontario Arts Council and the Canada Council for the Arts for our publishing program. The financial support of the Government of Canada is also gratefully acknowledged.

Table of Contents

Foreword

Always pure, and often rarefied, the poems of Kay Smith present the reader with the visions emanating from her ontological imagination. In her mind she saw a strange conflation, blending images and metaphors and symbols, all appearing without any choice—occasionally, in her early poems, causing her to forego clear connections, and to fracture ordinary grammar, to produce a super-modern language, which could cause her readers difficulty. Even many of her later poems still surprise us with their choice of diction. Some believed Smith was a mannerist, but no one doubted her intelligence, and no one thought she was not serious. In time she came to simplify her syntax, but she never abjured images—not even private fragments in her mind—and what they meant to her great love of being. Images are often metaphoric; or they might be truly anagogic: showing readers right reality, a *sui generis* of final forms.

A good example is the following, the highly focused ending of 'Girl Napping':

> On waking, if the world is a paper hoop, treason
> against the ache to be, will she leap through the real,
> kneel with the stone and sail with the gull?

That is, is what the girl sees in her dreams *more* real than what the world pretends is real? And will she have the courage to break through her consciousness and ordinary senses? Kay Smith had that courage, in abundance, for she knew each poem is transcendent, something to be *found* in ideal being, as a vision of imagination.

What, then, are the stone and gull she sees? They are not vehicles of other things. They are not bodies of abstruse abstractions. Neither stone nor gull has any meaning. Each one is exactly what it is, and nothing other than its simple self. Both stone and gull are images of *being*—what the world is in reality, where one will kneel before the Throne of God, and one can fly because one feels so free. Kay Smith was always painfully aware the world she wanted seemed to be a dream, but she believed desire might come true, because what she imagined overwhelmed her with its beauty and its timelessness. On Grand Manan, the island where she summered, off New

Brunswick's southern Fundy coast, she found a treasure trove of images. In 'Shells' she tells us, sadly, she is one

> who always seems poised on the verge
> of breaking   breath held
> between wonder and weeping

Being is both pure and wonderful, and Kay Smith always tried to write us there, by showing us the world that she imagined. She once said she should have been a painter — homage, maybe, to her good friend Miller Brittain, from the art scene on Prince William Street, whose probing portrait of her in her thirties shows her gazing at eternity, with wistful passion in her poet's eyes.

To be is to be ultimately whole, beyond becoming, satisfied forever. In 'I Cradle a Stone in My Hand', another poem found on Grand Manan, Kay Smith rejoices in the stone's perfection, realizing eons passed to form it, as it now is, washed up from the sea. And then she pauses to ask God a question:

> How long, O Lord, how long before we know
> In ourselves and our world
> The full flowering of the human?

This simple question — let alone the answer — takes us to the realm of metaphysics, or, in Kay Smith's terms, religious faith, from which arose her own poetic myth of Images as Elements of Being, where the Word and Comforter prevail. She was a questing Christian all her life, but what she found was sometimes difficult to satisfy her constant need *to be*, for Christians are susceptible to sin, while being is poetic but amoral. In her poems light and shadows clash, and light exists in her imagination as perfection in the universe — regardless of whatever form it takes. It should be noted that in Kay Smith's poems darkness is not opposite to light, for darkness is potentiality for being to appear in sudden glory. From it leaps the morning sun each day! Light streams from God, and shadows stream from light. From God to light to shadows flows the world. To be redeemed one must reverse this flow. If light is being, shadows are non-being, what prevents us taking faithful action and achieving poetry and love. In 'Footnote to The Lord's Prayer' Kay Smith tells us that we must encounter and defeat the Shadow of non-being to fulfill the raging ache *to be*, what she calls there 'deliverance' from sin.

In youth Kay Smith was Puritanical, and therefore painfully aware of evil. One of her best poems is 'O Light', in which she pleads with God to postpone coming to administer a final judgement, in the fullness of illumination, till we know how deeply we have sinned:

> make but the thought of light a tiger leaping and deadly,
> to turn us back to the cities the evil of our minds has builded,
> prey to the red-mouthed harlots in the streets of our wishes,
> tearing our paper hearts, littering pavements and alleys
> on the way to cupid-rocked nests in the neon-veined west ...
> among the hearts and flowers kissed skull on the pillow,
> where arrowed to the sheet the body of our darkness grows.

Smith chooses sex for light to castigate, when it is casual and meaningless, and yet she praises sex as love's true being. Light is present as a blessing then. The lover is a visitor divine, and when the woman finds him in her bed, she *jubilates*, as Smith would come to say. 'Light opens like a lily,' she declared in 'Orchard Morning', later in her life, when she remembered love's first joyous moments. Smith suggests that making love is sacred and the final cause of being human. And, unlike the stones upon the beach, we do not have to wait for untold ages. *We can be completely human now*—no need for oceanic time to form us. All we have to do is fall in love, and keep the faith that has rewarded us with life as real as any youthful vision.

Ah, but wonder often turns to weeping. In a sequence of love poetry—that I would call *A Trip to Love and Grief*—Kay Smith describes the passionate affair she had with a man she met in Europe on a summer touring holiday, when she was in the middle of her life. These lyrics, or the greater part of them, appeared in *At the Bottom of the Dark*. The poems in this sequence are divided into what the lovers did in Florence, Nice and other European cities and the heartache that the poet felt when she returned to Canada alone: the joy of being, then the pain of losing. 'Florence' is intensely beautiful, the finest poem Kay Smith ever wrote. Its hauntingly repeated images suggest a story of great loneliness appreciated by great tenderness. One can never read this charming lyric without wanting to read it again:

> Do you remember walking alone
> on a hot summer night in Florence
> in the crowded streets in the darkness
>
> I remember your walking alone
> I remember your eyes the look in your eyes
> that told me there was only you
> no one but you in an ocean of darkness
>
> and I was weeping all the tears of my life
> as I walked with friends and laughed with them
> in the narrow streets in the darkness
>
> There was a child who lost his mother
> in the darkness   there was a man
> who lost   who can say what he lost
> as precious as his life in the darkness
>
> if I could find for him what he lost
> and give it back I would rejoice
> though I walked alone in the narrow streets
> alone in the narrow streets in the darkness

It was the lover's inability—or was it just his maddening reluctance?—to express his love for her in words that aggravated Kay Smith's loneliness as she recalled his summertime embraces. 'In This Season of Frosts and Separation' brings to life her sorrow in his silence:

> When under your kindling touch,
> I burned in your arms like a forest,
> There was no need of words.
>
> Now in this season of frosts and separation
> I burn alone, a single torch
> Among the leafless columns.

I beg the silence to speak in tongues
Of crystal meanings that could not be
Save for your absence and my burning.

In the nights alone I cannot beg
The words I need for healing,
And so instead I ask for crystal meanings.

Existentially created *being*—tragic grief when lovers fall apart—reveals how grim reality can be. And Kay Smith's yearning for the Comforter to speak in tongues and show her 'crystal' visions, which transcend the words of understanding, shows the price one sometimes pays *to be*.

To Kay Smith's credit, she did not complain. In 'Postscript' she declares about her lover, 'I am brimful with that wordlessness, / All that our bodies said and heard,' which puts to shame her other suitors' words, the emptiness of all their metaphors. In 'Orchard Morning' she sums up the image that her lover left her for all time:

as god I saw him
as lion lying down with lamb and
(most poignantly and mercifully)
ordinary-extraordinary
man

As the poem 'Postscript' tells us plainly, all her adult life Smith was romantic. She had many boyfriends, as she called them, but they did not satisfy her soul. The man in Europe was the one she loved, with all her being, all her vital light. And she continued loving him till death. She said, 'I am an unclaimed precious woman.' Anyone who knew her would agree.

Michael Oliver
Saint John, NB

The poet's eye, in a fine frenzy rolling,
Doth glance from heaven to earth, from earth to heaven,
And as imagination bodies forth
The forms of things unknown, the poet's pen
Turns them to shapes, and gives to airy nothing
A local habitation and a name.

—*A Midsummer Night's Dream,* V, i, 12–17

Deep-Sea Diver

Experience is
the diving board
from which she leaps
to find the Word,
bracing litheness
on the edge of laughter
the diver seems
a tight-rope dancer,
then sudden tautness
and she curves
to cut with youngness
the plastic waves;
under water
under the breakers
under the mind
there are no wakers,
no wakers calling
Time to get up,
to comb out
the intimate quirk,
drink from
the common cup;
no familiar tool
of a tree
Outside the window
to sew up the gaping
wound in the walking
shadow, sleep
having cut out
the personal core
as she lay on her pillow,
now a stranger handles
her private woe
that lies about
on the top of the dresser

* * *

But under water
the personal flows
into impersonal
fluid prose,
cutting consonants
of starfish hands
join body's meaning
with ribboned sands,
on water tablet
the hands are spelt
ten letters
rippling like velvet,
the sharp-tongued shoulder
fans to a vowel,
unsyllabled sound
of the ocean swell
blunts the ear
like a fish-hook curled
to catch the single
rainbow word;
but nothing separate
articulates,
water and flesh
have become mates,
there at the foot
of the tall wave
image and looker
melt in the coral
cave fold
over fold in
the flowing grave.

So the question is
will the diver rise
the unsyllabled sea
sound in her eyes

(for the found is wordless
the sound no sound
to ensnare in a private
cage or plant
in a plot of ground)
and will she slip over
with the sea's slide
over the door sill
satisfied,
no symbol to prove her
no souvenir
to show to the neighbours
or put away
in a drawer

O Light

O light that grows in eyes purged with the tears of agony,
come to us not yet, not till the horror of our sin has flowered in us,
for we must show unequivocally that diseased darkness loves us;
make but the thought of light a tiger leaping and deadly,
to turn us back to the cities the evil of our minds has builded,
prey to the red-mouthed harlots in the streets of our wishes,
tearing our paper hearts, littering pavements and alleys
on the way to cupid-rocked nests in the neon-veined west …
among the hearts and flowers kissed skull on the pillow,
where arrowed to the sheet the body of our darkness grows.

When morning comes without fanfare, a cool fact in the east,
and no crumb of a positive left in the cupboard,
only scraps of despair, memorial to the feast
that leaves us leaner than ever, our hunger keen as a sword,
when with nothing remaining to feed the maw of our night,
eyes face their terrible fear, the naked light,
then will the humble ribs with a flash through flesh
take cleanly the light, their glad answer of yes
held in the high window that looks both in and out,
that frames the whole frame of a man and makes with the serving sun
a coronet of his brow, but not yet, O light, not now.

The Eye of Humility

In the dream, in the charmed dream we are flying
not as a kite held at the other end by hand of flesh,
rich in the smell of grass and colts munching
in the sunned field and air smooth as milk,
but with the limbs and torso webbed with a metal boldness,
scorning the matters of earth, the mole, the blind mole's wisdom,
bodies under the tree and a sweetness clouding the tongue.

In the dream, in the charmed dream, we alone have motion,
the world below a still life bathed in a green pre-thunder light,
hand on the wheel stuck like a fly in syrup,
the shovel raised never to fall, eyelid staid as a stone.

In the awakening, in the crash of awakening,
the heart is jolted into its eye,
the ancient oak in the dream an acorn
crowds into the eye,
the seed of Adam enters, Man of Sorrows,
with the eternal stars of wounds in His thigh;
in the dream, in the charmed dream we were flying
out of mind, who now are grounded with the slow root
in the invaded womb of time.

When a Girl Looks Down

When a girl looks down out of her cloud of hair
And gives her breast to the child she has borne,
All the suns and the stars that the heavens have worn
Since the first magical morning
Rain through her milk in each fibre and cell of her darling.

Hand baring the gift touches the hidden spring,
Source of all gifts, the womb of creation;
From the wide-open door streams the elation
Shaping all things, itself shapeless as air,

That models the nipple of girl, of bud, the angel
Forms unscrolling their voices over fields of winter,
That whittles the ray of a star to a heart's splinter
For one lost in his palace of breath on the frozen hill,
Flying the big-bellied moon for a sail.

And releases the flood of girl, of bud, of the horn
Whose music starts on a morning journey.
In mother, child and all, the One-in-the-many
Gathers me nearer to be born.

Integration

So hard not to name it, not to use wooing speech,
crying, 'Loveliness, come, lost child in the casket,'
with seeking hands folded, waxen and quiet,
unwanted at the ends of delicate stems,
crying, 'Come.'

So hard not to kneel down
at the edge of this silence
to see if the image is there,
where the dream of Icarus in a handful of feathers
lies with features perfectly still.

Not the eyes of the flier recall
to their gaze climbing up the blue stalk of the air.
not It to call back from its traffic in bone
for there is no separate existence for it anymore,
but It walks in the limbs when they move upon mountains
and is all that the hands may do for growing things.

Words for a Ballet

Wilderness is not desert, wilderness is mirrors.
When the sun burns the glass the image performs,
Sun-worshipper makes an arch of hands, flows a river,
And conjures in columns of bone white birds in storms.

He coaxes, cajoles, dances the sun yet light
But gilds the dance, his heart is no gold trumpet.
Guess the time and season when wings collect from flight
In a group of static birds lodged in a sweetheart locket.

Wilderness is not desert, no devil leaps boulders,
Wilderness reflects a morning of April,
In matching sash of blue the artist changes gender,
Under rocketing bush of hair the dancer virginal

Spends her wandlike beauty in the lake of your eyes,
Fetches a cowl of cloud with her twigfine fingers,
And when the curving limbs publish their delicate lies
Covers them with the candour clinging of the air.

All seems but nothing is in that country of mirrors,
Costumes change the contours but not the heart
No simulated sunlight of stages discovers.
When will the lovely honest darkness start,

And wilderness become itself the map of a journey
Where the shoes of false selves travel the road,
But the discoverer never moves from the centre of that city
That a sudden dawn will light in the darkness of God?

from Footnote to The Lord's Prayer

[Our Father]

Our Father when morning walks on ocean,
when trees answer the light with birds in their speech,
when light turns gull wings all but transparent
for the wader in light seeking weightless to swim;
Our Father when morning goes down to the children
poised on the fringe of ocean and gathering off
the Point the endless brightness of seas to their mouths'
crescents, the knowledge and nearness of far that flows
with their movements at home in this flowing world;
Our Father when the common flower cleanses,
terse with the wit of sky and earth in its root,
when grass points to creation's inwardness,
trembling with a million shining clues in the light,
brushing the naked feet with living poems,
washing the multiple wishes with Oneness that is;
Our Father when morning walks on ocean,
Our Father in the shapes and voices of things,
In the featureless light around the heart, the cradle,
Son of light for the darkness in everyman.

[Deliverance]

When, when will deliverance come?

Go down, go down, proud daughter,
go down with your limbs that burn like the sun,
go down in the night to the water,
to the depths of your sorrow, go down, child,
to the cold, stinging depths of your sorrow,
go down when the moon burns like a wound,
go down to the Shadow on the water.

• • •

In the lighted towers of Manhattan,
in the cocktail glasses of Long Island,
in the tenement kitchens of the nations,
where light screams on faces,
in the bedrooms under the eaves
where candles bend to the wind,
in the blindwhiteness of surgery,
in the drunkard's eyes on the curbstone,
in the waxy white of breasts
under the lips of lover,
in the uncanny white of magnolias,
in the topaz light of eyes
beading the dark of forests,
in the light of the scientist's brain,
from light, lights, the light
streams forever the Shadow.

[Thy Kingdom]

Thy Kingdom
to keep our hunger whole
till the lights go on in the theatre
till the speaker throws out his lariat
for the last time to sharpen
the instinct for ghosts in us
who are not yet born
as they peddle their singing
birds in crystal cages

Thy Kingdom
to guard in us what is real
the dream to live in Thy Kingdom
finished at last with shadows

Girl Napping

Through the cracked blind the Saturday sunlight sifts,
street noises festoon her limbs and sprout in her veins,
child of chaos, she hides in these, then drifts
through a jungle growth down shrill green lanes.
Ah, the scarlet burning of eyes in the leaves, the mists
that form in funeral lilies and fall like the rain!
On the pillow the small face smeared with cream
takes with bland innocence the dream.

The dream scatters defenses with ripping claws,
even the cloak of fear falling from head to feet,
to the potent voice of the seed, its cry that draws
the sun to its womb in the blind beginning of wheat,
the silk of her nays dribbles from streaming jaws,
what seemed intimately hers is rent like meat,
all is scattered like chaff the wind blows.
The small face on the pillow knows?

If she knows in the dream, is there hope for her scattered?
Question answers question. Does season follow season?
Does earth waste a single leaf battered
on her breast? Nature's rhythm is reason,
the law no meddling hand has ever shattered.
On waking, if the world is a paper hoop, treason
against the ache to be, will she leap through the real,
kneel with the stone and sail with the gull?

Again with Music

Now that the rain is spent,
Trees and the purple-headed timothy and the tall grasses
Are all netted over with seed pearls.
Far as the eye can reach the sea is pale as a pearl,
The air a pool of stillness,
And so still the wild roses their petals make porcelain faces.

From leaf to leaf a raindrop slips,
Stillness upon stillness.

And sprawling over the living grass and the roses,
A dead apple tree with beauty in its bare bones,
Never to put forth again a pink and white cloud of witnesses,
Suddenly blossoms with yellow birds in its grey limbs,
And is almost alive again with music.

Love, O Love, let the birds happen to me.
Let the wild, sweet voices remember me.

Autobiography

Death wore a golden arm
When he struck my brother down,
And I but a seed growing
In the dark of my mother's womb.

All music hushed
In the golden horn of the street
As they carried him into the house
And shut the summer out.

Winter stopped mailed
Over my mother's years,
And froze the honey in the comb,
And with a breath her tears.

All the birds of her blood
Were trapped in his black frost.
He slipped the bolt on her door
And blocked all roads to her heart.

And I in the dark of the cave,
A dumb and a blind seed,
Swelled in a double dark
Of birth and my mother's grief.

And when I reached for the sun,
And cradled it like a gift,
She saw the bolt fly back,
And the spell of winter lift.

Yet in those sailing days
When I sailed the ship of my flesh,
On a sudden the flying green world
Would jolt to a stop in a flash.

And a stranger in a billowy cloak,
Who wore a golden arm,
Crowded the deck in black,
Shielding my brother's form,

In the folds of his dusky cape
Caressed the flaxen head,
And smiled into my eyes,
As though I too were dead.

Who in his fungus of years
Can feel a child's sorrow,
Hearing in a mother's heart-beats
The pulse of its own tomorrow?

Or who with the world in his blood,
A figure in the mad myth,
Can guess the magnet that draws
In the winsome smile of Death?

Who even feebly can tell
The mourning of earliest morning,
When floating planets of dew
Snap with a black sleeve passing?

At such a time I lived
As out of myself as in,
Dogging the hero of legend,
Clever, blithe, without sin.

I was the far-off alien
Unworthy to be seen by the
Boy with his hand in his mother's,
The golden son of a queen.

In the logic of guilt was born
The thought that my life was spun
From the body of his death,
A dark thread punished with sun.

What right had I to live,
As a castaway to rove,
Groping in a foreign tongue,
On the shores of my mother's love?

All that I could be
Was a tumbler in front of Death,
To dazzle her from his smile,
To cartwheel in his path.

And I, because I knew
The charm of Death still held her,
Walked into his net,
Became his fearful lover.

I could not bear her grief:
I wanted only my love
To dance her into a wave,
To fit her like a glove.

I wanted the legend of roses
To be our permanent home,
Where beauty walked enchanted,
And no rude waker to come.

But one with x-ray sight
Entered the heart of the myth,
Stripped me to the bone,
And left the beginning of self.

In the place of beasts and angels
I build my permanent home,
Endure the changing weathers,
Honour the rose and the stone.

In the sea around my island,
I float my little lights
For love to find a way
To last me through the nights.

Family Group

I look out the bus window at the grey rain,
at houses flush with the pavement in a shabby street,
at trees unstirred by the calendar fact of April;
in our city spring has a hard birth.

The bus stops for a boy in faded blue jeans,
who looks seventeen not a day older,
and a girl a year younger perhaps, wearing
too thin a coat for the still wintry weather.

With one hand the boy grips a carton,
and with the other a paper bag of groceries;
the girl carries in her arms a crying infant,
the blanket worn from many washings.

The face of the young mother is grave but serene
as she cradles in her arms the child whose crying
is the smallest sound of grief as sad as the rain;
the young father sighs as he balances his parcels.

There seems nothing to remember about this little group
unless it is the pathos of their youth and poverty,
yet I think I'll remember them against falling rain
and unbudded trees in a shabby street.

To such as these life opens once her secret heart,
and what weeps now was once a breath of ecstasy.

Beach Scene

The blond lifeguard walks among the blue water hillocks at sea's edge,
And with the prongs of his fork lifts a jellyfish into exile
On the fawn sands. The children polished with light
Like water-sleek seals, explode in brilliant asterisks of delight.

The purple corpse lies on the sand, opaque glass.
It could be a paperweight with a white ribbon bow design at the centre.

Nothing to do but bury the body.
A waferthin boy with a head like a sunbeam
Pours fistfuls of pale sand on the victim.
And the children dance, dance, dance
Under the ice cream clouds by the summer sea,
And nothing is clearer than their laughter
Or purer than their pleasure except the sea,
The murdering sea.

I Cradle a Stone in My Hand

I cradle a stone in my hand,
A black stone, shining wet and smooth as the flank of a wave,
Shaped and grained by wind and tide.
How many aeons have brought it to perfection?
I rejoice in its being at home in the universe
And in the wholeness of its being.
Who would think a stone could nourish a dream,
Its cool curve like a phrase completing a poem?
How long, O Lord, how long before we know
In ourselves and our world
The full flowering of the human?

Return to Innocence

This poem is a thimbleful
          of happiness
if you are looking for more
          meaning
          in symbols
mole wisdom in tunnels
          stop here

This poem is an eyeful
          of teal-blue sea
an opening parasol of gulls
          over
red-roofed fish houses
and curlings of surf on
          blond sands
and two friends who surface
from their separate lives
          walk together
          in the poem
after twenty years of being apart

They hold between them
the crystal of memory
          seeking their young
          enchanted faces
where wild beasts gaze as bland as milk
          where leaf never falls
          or nest is plundered
          where hand in hand
they walk forever in the heart of the green wood

Holland

I lived in a dream of bells
forming and fading
golden and silver fruits
on the tree of my flesh

I sailed in the dream
on windless canals
in a spell of light

Beautiful flaxen-haired
children ran through the dream
flying their kites great birds on fire
in sunlit space

All the while I was unaware
of a dark figure
standing outside the margin
the real magician
who could make the dream disappear
with a touch of his very real hand
or change it to an abstract of water and lights

Such was his magic
that I a woman with too real a body
to disappear
move now in a landscape bleak as a moon
while you the magician
become the figure in the dream
sailing on windless canals
in a spell of light

Cologne

From the cathedral of dark lace
We walked, a little crowd of strangers
Window shopping in the night,
Each locked within his separate world,
Hedged in with laughter and the words we spoke,
When suddenly, you, of all most strange,
Were walking with a wild bird beating in your hand,
The sound of muffled thunder in the place between the words.

I think of ice in springtime breaking in the night,
And all along my northern river
Hammered by the moon,
Men and women smiling from their sleep
To dream how soon the winter-punished earth
Will blossom for a season like their flesh.

On the Way to Heidelburg

The windshield pricked with silver pinpoints of the rain
Reflects the green of a young cherry orchard.
As you light your pipe, a flame
Burns briefly in the mirrored leaves of green.

When your absence becomes the incredible fact
Will the flame you have kindled die in me
Or will it consume my last green leaf?

Somewhere after Innsbruck

In an old city
        a flight of pigeons
wings molten in sunlight

Your eyes look down
  into my ferncool darkness
              then
 the sudden ascension in fire

Florence

Do you remember walking alone
on a hot summer night in Florence
in the crowded streets in the darkness

I remember your walking alone
I remember your eyes the look in your eyes
that told me there was only you
no one but you in an ocean of darkness

and I was weeping all the tears of my life
as I walked with friends and laughed with them
in the narrow streets in the darkness

There was a child who lost his mother
in the darkness   there was a man
who lost   who can say what he lost
as precious as his life in the darkness

if I could find for him what he lost
and give it back I would rejoice
though I walked alone in the narrow streets
alone in the narrow streets in the darkness

In These Nights

In these nights fragments of mirrors
Glitter with inklings
Of our separate features,
Our different lives.
Nor are clocks benign or silent,
But we make love to another kind of time
Under their threatening hands.
And a fire burns,
Seeking to melt and join, though vainly,
These granite solitudes,
Yours and mine....

Sometimes Bitterness Shaped Your Words

Sometimes bitterness shaped your words;
for instance, that night three of us sat in the roof garden,
beneath us the palms of Nice and the ocean
— not a rustle in the darkness —
overhead the summer stars beating like golden pulses.
You spoke of the Suez crisis, having to get out of Egypt
and leave behind a prosperous business;
gall flowed in your words.

But when you looked down at the city beneath us
and said, 'Alexandria was like this,
beautiful with its trees and its flowers!'
I knew you had lost more than money,
more than the beauty of flowers.

And once as the smoke curled from your pipe,
and you looked at the stars, naming them,
I turned my back and I looked up at the stars
to hide my eyes from yours.

Later that night when there were only the two of us,
the other still sipping his drink under the stars,
your words stopped altogether.
They had become the bittersweet of your lovemaking;
still I ache with the memory. It lingers in my flesh
like the fragrance in a house
where flowers are still fresh
after those who live there
have closed the door and departed.

Eyes

When your eyes told me more than your words,
I lowered mine, fearing to snare some secret joy
Skimming on fragile wings the witches' wood.
How could I intrude on shape of pain or solitude
I had no right to share in darkness or the bright summer air,
Or dove from Christ's strong hand
Crowning some ruined tower on lonely skies?

But when your eyes were golden with laughter,
My eyes borrowed their sun and were not shy
To enter yours, as if I had never known in myself
Anything but morning, jewel-hung grasses
And liquid bird voices. Then your happiness
Was the most exquisite gift my eyes could hold.

In These Autumn Days

In these autumn days
a spinning of golden coins
        fruit is sweetest

Hurry to me in your thoughts
already the leaves are rustling
        in the parks
    like dead butterflies

In This Season of Frosts and Separation

When under your kindling touch,
I burned in your arms like a forest.
There was no need of words.

Now in this season of frosts and separation
I burn alone, a single torch
Among the leafless columns.

I beg the silence to speak in tongues
Of crystal meanings that could not be
Save for your absence and my burning.

In the nights alone I cannot beg
The words I need for healing,
And so I ask instead for crystal meanings.

Where You Have Never Been

Why do you walk all day
Beside me here where you
Have never been, where
The tall firs and spruces
Make stylized implacable
Angels and the sculptured
Snow is cold, cold as my bed
Or a Puritan heaven.
A winter bird divides the air
With a single note sharp as my hunger,
And a lemon sun touches the snow
With fingers of pale light between bare poplars.

Why do you lie beside me here
Where you have never been,
In this northern silence of darkness
Glittering with stars sharp as my hunger,
In this bed where, in your absence,
I feast on your ghostly presence,
And burn like frost between the sheets
As white and cold as the snow
Of my own, my vast country, my bed
Of silence and stars and black-on-whiteness.

Postscript

One said when I was young and gold with summer,
No other man will want you more,
I want you as a wounded man wants water.
I wept, slipped from his arms and out his door
Into the sad summer moonlight
And heard the river sighing on the shore.

The One said when I was young and young no longer,
As season followed season and year followed year.
I think of you as dark and cool and deep
My darling. I fall and fall through space in you—
A falling star…

Another said not long ago when words like snow
Sifted through skeletons of grass and flower,
You are the image of light on thresholds of darkness.
Let light invade my darkness from head to toe.

But you who are water and space and light to me
Spoke no single word to lift me like a bird,
And I am brimful with that wordlessness,
All that our bodies said and heard.

The Bird of Sorrow Would Sing

If I could learn to know sorrow were chosen,
The bird of sorrow would sing in my tree.

Such knowledge would strip me of heavy armour,
And the sun dress me in tissues of gold.

The wild rose would light its flaming torches,
And my phoenix heart burn in its incense.

Where, bitter, I wandered through dry places,
Summer would drip its honeycomb on my mouth.

The blue sea would stand up and clash its cymbals
For me to dance in my worshipping bones.

And my spirit looking out on a birthday morning
Would receive coloured jewels from the fingers of grasses.

If I could learn to know sorrow were chosen,
The bird of sorrow would sing in my tree.

Pegasus and Swan

On sky as polished as a shell,
Two clouds in profile, motionless;
One, a plumy Pegasus;
A swan, the other, beautiful
As no earthly sculpture is,
Gifted with motion like a gull,
As if to fly, as if to sail,
On the brink of metamorphosis.

They pause, considering the change
To other symbols, other forms
With which the burning fancy swarms
When given liberty to range,
Yet with that liberty remain
A winged horse without a rider,
A marble swan so fair a glider,
No hand could ever coax or rein.

Meanwhile, fashioned for reflection,
We wait, the summer sea and I,
To faithfully record the sky,
Each pearly tone, each cool inflection,
And shaken with the poet's rage,
And shaded by the wing of death,
I strive with every darkening breath
To lure these shiners to my page.

Morning, Grand Manan

And morning a great sea-shell that I may enter
for something performs a breath of miracle
I give the slip to flesh through spirit's keyhole

And the three roving tenses cease to travel
their three paths merging in this footless air
that sieves to purest essence the buoy's bell

Sky makes with sea as they melt one pearl
a boat far out on sky seems to sail
silver grey and beige the sands swirl

Loops curls crescents splashed with greens
sea-weed sings in tongues of three sheens
parrot asparagus and bronze-tinged

Dew-white water mirrors on sands glimmer
where pale clear honey suns gild gulls
and sandpipers flicker on feet gilt-hinged

And there by the tide on a rock pampered
in toasted gold brown weed a heron culls
the silver cord of silence with his bill

Then on slow sensuous wings rises
shakes the sea-sky pearl to a blue blur
sinks in distances the eye prizes

Ringed with here and now it cannot bear
but I am filled to wordless overflowing
purged to the clarity of a single tear

For love shines salt with everlasting
reflects the moment's sky, the joy, the fear,
ringing its towers of bells on climbing air

You in the Feathery Grass

You in the feathery grass, dropping the nubbled berry
into the thick bowl, you who linger in country roads
with naked feet, knowing the heat and texture of the steaming dust,
you, woman, standing in the doorway filling with twilight,
feeling a soft head on your breast, a harder pushing against your thigh,
you, hired boy, sitting on the snake fence in the summer moonlight,
thinking of the crazy fiddle under the hanging lamps,
the city guys with laughter in their eyes like dry sticks burning,
thinking of the musty sweetness of hay in barns,
with knotted breath thinking of the bodies of women;

and you, moving on the wild March sky
as on cloud-driven mornings since time began to form
in your boy's mind, moving on the plunging sky
with the long sweeping rhythm of a scythe through tall grasses,
hoping behind the closed face for warm days soon and sowing,
feeling against the blunt hand familiar hardness of seed
like hail falling on the ready ground;

you, all of you who know affinity with dust, speak it soon,
scatter the seed of your knowing quickly,
reckon it up in debts and credits,
have it written in the yellowing account book on the kitchen mantel,
before dust chokes the single outline,
blurs the individual mouth.

That Something May Be Found

That something may be found I make a poem.
I break from the shell of habit, my home,
leaving fear, the old crone, nodding by the cold ashes.

Near the door Eyes compel so large and clear
a walking out that clothed simply in being
I try to deserve the white lashes of the daisy,
the tapering body of grass in the wind,
and stones washed in sunlight.

That the secret may be found I become a hunter
in a poem, seeking the lost child who followed
the moonlight into the wood.

In the wood and in the waste places under
a half-moon we are very wonderful,
curved like a bow over being ourselves and alone,
moving when we move like a half-moon.

That something may be found I make a poem.

Summer Night, Grand Manan

How pleasant to slip down the gentle hill of sleep
Under the winking stars in the summer dark,
The moon laying her lacquer fan on the sea,
And folding in her white as waterfall sleeves
Silent houses and sleeping faces of children like rosy shells,
The two white churches dreaming shoulder to shoulder in the village street;
How pleasant to feel one's clamorous flesh slip into moonlight
Between two cool drops of drowsy birdsong.

And pleasant it is to wake in the night
To the multitudinous tongues of the rain,
Listening until one's very bones issue the sweet sound;
The window suddenly brightens, cars of fishermen go plunging
Through the rain for the weir tide is running,
Tires on pavements make suspirations like surf's,
And headlights, great cats' eyes, drink the rainy darkness,
Glow a moment then are gone,
Leaving the darkness larger and deeper,
While crowding to the heart's door,
The fluting voices of the rain fashion a clearer,
Lovelier and oh, lonelier music than before.

The Skeleton in the Closet

The skeleton was in the closet
she hung it there after the ravens
had picked it clean
she asked herself
What could be neater
for my narrow closet
what could be cleaner
than bones stripped bare
The skeleton was in the closet
and she was in the kitchen
she hummed and stirred the porridge
with a wooden spoon
What could be safer
than a skeleton in a closet
all but forgotten behind the door
what could be tamer
than a skull with empty sockets
what less accusing
than a skull without a tongue
what could be safer
than a skeleton in a closet
for one whose secret pocket hides the key

From time to time the season winter
she unlocked the door
when nothing but the moon
peeked in her window
and every time the bones looked whiter
than the time before
but afterwards she always locked the door
As the clock ticked away
and the calendar months shrivelled
she visited less often
her prisoner in the closet
though sometimes she fingered
lovingly the key

* * *

One day looking up
from the garment she was patching
she saw surprised that winter had ended
the world was a lamb frisking in a green meadow
and a tree was opening shiny leaves
like a girl's mouth for kisses
    That night upon her narrow bed
    she dreamed of openings
    those of petals virgins envelopes
    containing lovers' letters tombs
    cocoons windows doors wombs
    and children's round luminous eyes
    floating on thin stalks in darkness
    over and around the narrow bed
    where she was lying
Suddenly the dream shattered
the closet door was opening
how could it a locked door
the key hidden in her secret pocket
    But the senses took what the mind rejected
    she could feel its breath hear breathing
    Its breathing? His? Some passing stranger's?
    God present? the Devil perhaps?
Whoever or whatever
full length she felt a weight upon her
hands burned up the gown of frost
covering her from neck to ankle
then reached the flesh then something
that was not the flesh
not even the bright moon could classify
nor she could name
but she felt it like her heart
as it ascended on strong and steady wings
the steep abyss where she was falling
and JUBILATE sang a voice and it was hers

When morning came she woke
to see the imprint of a head
beside hers on the pillow
and all the windows and the doors
except the skeleton's
were open to a silence deeper
than the silence of the snow that
once had wound cold arms around her
Trembling she rose
and in her nakedness and terror
tried to open that closed door
but it was locked
and when she somehow found the strength
to find the key where it had lain a lifetime
in her secret pocket and the strength to put
the key where it belonged
the door swung wide
and hanging staring at her
from within the closet
nothing

And JUBILATE sang the sun through all her windows
And JUBILATE sang the bird outside her door
And JUBILATE sang the wound between her thighs

Symbol

I.

Growing older we are
overtaken it seems by the poignancy of symbols
even the body a symbol
eye   hand
especially the bird
soaring in blue space
on delicate framework of
bone and wing
or
fallen
a stone bird
on a stone statue
at the heart of a city of stone

II.

What might have been the poem
is the bird
diminishing
as
it
soars
to lose itself at last
in
blue wells
of
infinity

Old Women and Love

Drowning
no end to it

Yeats should have discovered Byzantium
as no country for old women
yet they refuse to die
they clutter up the earth
the blood of old women continues to cry out
to sing even to dance wildly in their veins
Sometimes the blood of an old woman rustles
like a startled bird when love's stealthy step
cracks the dry undergrowth in the frosty air
as if a firecracker were exploding

It seems that love is a hunter of undiscriminating taste
Women old enough to know better — though God is never old
  enough —
dream deeper and deeper into the wood
like the misty-eyed girls they once were
Suddenly one will stop astounded as the trap
love has set closes its steel jaws on a foot of frail bones

This morning very early in this silent house of sleepers
when my eyes opened from the mercy of my own darkness
the world came at me like a blow
Its beauty burned gold in every resurrected leaf
burned with a still flame   Spring never relents
What was I doing here?   What *was* I doing here?
Behind the house the trees slept paired in their cool shadows

At night an old woman on her narrow bed
probing the dark with a stubborn mind
demanding answers she knows she will not find
tends with a fierce joy the unextinguished embers
of a not so temperate love

The Healing

The last breath spun to breaking
and the torture of clocks ended
all the wounds heal over
with the new skin of silence
shreds of life come together
in one seamless garment

From the streets of the interior
demented words have fled
Over the city of the sleeper
still as a stone bird's flight
the Dawning Word hovers
begins again to seek the image
in the face naked now as water

Remembering Miller

(for Miller Brittain)

Touching my face
with your artist's fingers,
you said one day when we were young:
Never be afraid of growing old,
you have such good bones.

Now I am old
but the bones do not comfort me.
Yours matter to you even less
for hollow as they are,
where you lie, the wind has no chance
to make music with them or conversation.

Dear friend, you do not need the bones,
music or conversation with the wind,
nor does the world.

Your new body is the work,
it is your presence among us,
celebrant upon canvas.
This life of yours
glows before our eyes
as once, in all its colours, cadences,
it leapt and danced
raged and wept,
and more than this
reached out beyond itself
and will do so
long after all of us lie where your body lies.

It was in the reaching beyond
I knew you best,
I know you in my bones.

Shells

Of all the beaches on the island
this has the most beautiful shells

they are broken

Broken they bring revelation
taking you into their innermost porcelain skin
to drown you in colours
far too elusive and subtle
for naming

The spiral within that turns on itself
with all but hair-thin and fragile precision
yet is strong to withstand the wind and the tides
of this sea
has a meaning for one
who always seems poised on the verge
of breaking   breath held
between wonder and weeping

Message from Florence

I

Beneath the burning blue Italian sky
this Baptistry: the sculptured hand of Christ
a stone nest found by a white pigeon,
sun-warmed, safe, still as the stone.

The bird is at home,
part of what it cannot know.
Nor can we know, though we may dimly
sense the hand that holds us,
inviolate in our mystery.

The tall tranquil figure
standing above the tourist throng
and sober citizens of Florence,
guards above a sculptured frieze
one of Ghiberti's marvelous bronze doors.
Garden of Paradise Michelangelo named it.

Here we find ourselves,
figures in the ancient dream
we still dream in all the narrow streets,
days and nights of our pilgrimage.

II

In the hollow of your *human* hand
my love,
I am like that bird
so much at home,
yet sudden presentiment
gnaws at my peace.
I tremble, fear in you strength to endure
beyond your need of me.
Let me leave now before Time the Enemy
translates me:
Bird of stone.

Even in Absence

Pale and thin as barley water
is this light to which I wake.
If I close my eyes again,
all the blossoming spring
gathers under the lids.
Young swallows beneath the eaves
open their beaks to be fed;
I think of the throats of flowers.
I haven't heard such singing of birds
since that other haunted spring
of tissued greens and golds.

All torn to shreds
by the epileptic heart.

Now waking on this morning
in the spring of another year,
the world and I are rinsed in delicate water light.
The light begins to glow holy.

I think of you
as I break bread.
We touch even in absence.
Hungry, I am fed.

Lost

I have lost it
the moon up there
goldpiece in the sky

Who slipped it
into a secret pocket?
I know   I know

I have lost more
than the moon
oh, more than the moon

Than the fountaining
tree, its black lace caught
in the dying rose of the sun

Than the braided scents
in the clinging dusk
than the woven

bird-and-water notes
clear and delicate
in the darkening air

Moment by moment I shrink
lost at last ...
paler than the moon

Orchard Morning

In the first orchard morning
you wake to that divine visitor
in your bed.
Light opens like a lily.
Tangled in the sheet his body honours,
you marvel at the oceanic calm
upon him as he lies sleeping after love.
You see him as deliverer
as the sun kissing your cold breast.

I too had a lover
now yours,
one who will not rise to me from the depth of our embrace,
my legacy from him a three-fold vision;
as god I saw him
as lion lying down with lamb and
(most poignantly and mercifully)
ordinary-extraordinary
man

who, when from topmost tree
to earth I fell,
fed you my heart to keep you both well.

In That Light

Propped up on pillows
I look out into a once green world
preparing to go up in flames

The window opens to twin maples
the wind telling sad stories
This is the time when dusk begins
its delicate pressures
that the torn spirit cannot bear

Down from the house diffused light of
a pearl falls on the lake
I am in that light   falling

The truth is:
summer is over
no season will be summer again

Dusk

White paper face in a window
looking for the original out there
dusk deepens to smudge faces
lilac is the saddest colour in the sky

Even the self cloned
would be company
but the only mirror in the house
lies on the floor
shattered

If I could catch You Lord
the merest glimpse
as small as that of an eyelash
falling
and knew it was You

There would be no need of mirrors
or candle ends should light go out

About Kay Smith

Kay Smith spent almost her entire lifetime in the seaport of Saint John, New Brunswick. She was born there in 1911, and she died there in 2004. She grew up in a fine brick Uptown house, but as she came to her maturity, the Great Depression of the 1930s caused a downturn in her aspirations. She had hoped to study in New York, at the Academy of Dramatic Arts, supposing that she might become an actress. Though she studied drama for a summer at Columbia University, she was forced, like many of her friends — the painter Miller Brittain, for example — to return to Saint John penniless.

Back home, Kay Smith began to act in amateur productions of the Saint John Theatre Guild. By 1940 she had started teaching at a girls' school in Ontario, then two years later she came home again to take a posting at Saint John Vocational School, where she directed annual productions of the plays of Shakespeare — featuring her students in performance. These were highly celebrated in the local arts community. She stayed on there till 1970, and in retirement she sometimes taught at UNBSJ, giving courses in Creative Writing. Students liked her style of teaching, praising her for being serious and for welcoming discussions of their work; they also noticed she always carried books, and talked about them with enthusiasm.

Years before, when Kay Smith was a schoolgirl, she had heard Bliss Carman read his poems and decided she would be a poet. Or, she recognized she *was* a poet — born a poet, without any choice. Throughout the 1940s Kay Smith published poems in the finest journals in the country: *First Statement*, for example, and *Contemporary Verse*. She never married, and she never had a child. She lived, instead, for poetry and drama, and she was close friends with many painters, such as Miller Brittain and Jack Humphrey.

Also during these years in Saint John, Kay Smith and P.K. Page began a friendship that would last a lifetime, writing poems and discussing them and growing daily in their artistry. In 1951 Kay Smith's first book appeared. The slender *Footnote to The Lord's Prayer and Other Poems*, a series of religious meditations, is perhaps her most accomplished volume, although *At the Bottom of the Dark*, published twenty years later, might equal it in elegance of passion, as a series of erotic lyrics.

It was as a conscious modernist that Kay Smith began to write her poetry. That is, 'high modernism', written in fragments, in the style of T.S. Eliot, as contemplation of a central image, for its beauty or its mystery—not for its meaning as an allegory, or a symbol, or an ideation. Kay Smith's poems are original in using images as forms of being, not as signs of meanings or emotions. Images, to her, derive from dreams, for dreams are where we see reality. Although she often did use modern language—with its bleak impersonality—her poems sometimes can be more romantic than the fervid lyrics of Bliss Carman. Always they awaken, in the reader, complex intellectual emotions. She had very little interest in 1940s social modernism, much preferring, in her youth, religion, and then later, love's pure ecstasy.

Kay Smith's biography is fascinating, for she was a poet of perfection, radiating Images of Being, physical and metaphysical, in terms of light derived from God the Word, presenting love as Christian reverence, presenting love as sexual delight. Like William Blake, she was misunderstood for combining holiness and sex, and therefore she was often overlooked. Although she was supremely talented, Kay Smith did not promote her poetry, and seemed to be content with what she published, confident her legacy was solid, and good readers would admire her for having written soul-reflexive poems—as a poet, as a Christian dreamer, as a lover, as an aging woman.

A Bibliography

Other Canadians: New Poetry in Canada 1940–1946. Edited by John Sutherland. First Statement Press, 1947.

Footnote to The Lord's Prayer and Other Poems. First Statement Press, 1951.

Five New Brunswick Poets. Edited by Fred Cogswell. Fiddlehead Poetry Books, 1962.

At the Bottom of the Dark. Fiddlehead Poetry Books, 1971.

When a Girl Looks Down. Fiddlehead Poetry Books, 1978.

Again with Music: Seven Poems [a double gatefold pamphlet]. League of Canadian Poets, 1980.

The Bright Particulars: New and Selected Poems. Ragweed Press, 1987.

White Paper Face in the Window [a chapbook of five poems]. Purple Wednesday Society, 1987.

Editor's Acknowledgements

I wish to thank my wife, Patricia, for her absolute support throughout the preparation of this book: both in the generosity of her encouragement and in the application of her extraordinary research abilities—as well as in her fine suggestion of the epigraph!

Thanks are also owing to Bill and Mary Lou Joyce for their kind permission to use the copyright for this book from the Estate of Kay Smith.

Thanks go as well to Dr. Elizabeth McKim at St. Thomas University for her discussion of Kay Smith via the telephone.

Thanks also go to the Archives staff of the Saint John Free Public Library for providing access to Kay Smith's first—and very rare—book *Footnote to The Lord's Prayer and Other Poems*.

Thanks further go to Wendy (Shoots) Matheson at Dave Shoots, Bookseller, in Saint John, for helping us connect with Bill and Mary Lou Joyce in the first place.

And, right up to publication, thanks go to Stephanie Small at the Porcupine's Quill for her pleasant and diligent editorial assistance.